SURFING

written and photographed by Ed Radlauer

Bowmar Publishing Corp./Glendale, California

First Printing .... December 1968
Second Printing .... January 1970
Third Printing ...... August 1970
Fourth Printing .... July 1971

Water is great for sports. One water sport is drag boat racing. When this drag boat hits 180 miles per hour it throws out a big "rooster tail." Drag boats don't need waves. They make them.

Some people would rather make sand castles than rooster tails. Sand castle builders need lots of time and lots of wet sand. Castle builders don't want waves. Say, does anybody need waves?

Yes, there is a sport that needs waves. It's a sport that
lives on waves. It's a sport that must have waves, all kinds
of waves. You are right, it's surfing!

Surfing is not a new sport. People have been riding waves for hundreds of years. But hundreds of years ago they didn't have surfboards. No one knows when or how surfing was started. Was it a man whose boat sank?

Maybe this is how surfing started—body surfing. Many people still enjoy body surfing and there you don't even need a board. But you *do* need plenty of skill. It's you and your skill alone against all that water!

Those giant waves certainly make you feel small. Good body surfers know how long to stay in a wave and when to get out. A mistake will make you cut a groove in the sand—with your nose.

Here's a way to lie down on the job while surfing.
Use a bellyboard. Swim fins help you steer a bellyboard.
This kind of surfing isn't easy. Do swim fins make you
look like a fish?

You may lie down on the job while using a bellyboard, but you won't fall asleep. It takes skill to keep you, that board, and the surf in balance. The way you hold the board and your body gives you a good ride or a dumping into the surf.

Balance is important on a surfboard, too. It's so important that, without balance, you don't surf. Falling off a surfboard is easy. What is hard is keeping your balance and staying on. That's what surfing is all about!

There is much more to surfing than balance. Every good surfer has *tempo* and *style*. The way you control and move a board is your tempo. The way you balance yourself and hold your board in the surf is your style.

Every good surfer has his own style. *Trim* is part of style. Trim is the way you move your board along to match the speed of a wave. And if you don't match the wave's speed, you lose it.

There are many kinds of surf and each takes a different trim or style. A long hollow wave is sometimes called a *tube*. A tube can be good for a long ride if you catch it just where it begins to break.

A *shore break* can give a good ride, too. A shore break gives a long smooth wall that rides along as the wave breaks. Smooth water in the curve of a wave is called *glass.* Surfers like glass.

Surfing gives you a chance to meet your friends at the beach. Mike is showing his friends how the skeg comes out of his new surfboard. The skeg at the back of the board keeps you going straight. Without a skeg you might slide all over.

A wet surfboard is slippery. A special wax on the board
keeps it from getting too slippery. If you have the right
people to help, it's fun to wax your surfboard.

When you first go in the water, it seems cold. Some
surfers use a rubber wet suit to keep warm. The rubber
is soft and light. Sunshine helps you keep warm, too. But
as soon as the waves break, you forget about the cold.

Once in the water you paddle out to get that first wave. Waves come in to the beach in sets of two or three at a time. Surfers learn to watch the sets and pick the best waves for riding.

Why is it that the waves seem to stop as soon as you get out in the water? When the waves stop, the ocean turns into a giant parking lot for surfboards. Then there is nothing to do but wait.

As soon as the first set starts, you have to be up and ready to go. Now is the chance to feel how the surf is breaking and how fast the waves are moving. It's time to work out your style for the day.

If you are a very good surfer and very brave, you might try "shooting the pier." If you do try shooting the pier, you'd better know what you are doing. There is no telling what a wave will do as it roars under the pier.

Once there was a surfing contest and everyone came. That is, everyone came but the waves. Those in the contest had to show what they could do on small waves that mushed out. It isn't easy to ride a small wave before it mushes out.

In a contest you get points for your style and for special things you do on a surfboard. Hanging your toes over the end of the board is good for points. That's called "hanging five." Some people can "hang ten."

Is this a pretty good surf trick? No, it's a *wipe out.*
If you wipe out you lose your board and have to swim
for it. While you are swimming for your board, the other
surfers may be getting points.

An official of the surf club sits on the beach with an air horn. The air horn lets you know when to start and when to stop. Other officials and judges watch for style, tempo, and trim. They also watch for special tricks.

Most surfers surf just for fun. Each wave is different and new. Waves change from day to day and surfers keep working on their style and tempo. It seems you never learn all there is to know about surfing.

Sometimes surfers want to stay on the beach. There
are days when there is no glass, just *chop*. Rough water
is called chop. It gives you a rough ride and can be
dangerous.

All surfers look for hollow waves and water that looks
like glass. But on some days there is a lot of white water
or *soup*. A good surfer can ride in the white water. A
good surfer can ride almost anything.

Now, everybody knows you ride a surfboard with the skeg at the back. The skeg keeps your board straight. Everybody knows that! Well, almost everybody knows it.

If you are any kind of a boy friend, you will take your girl friend on a surfboard. This is *tandem surfing*. People say tandem surfing is the hardest way in the world to take a girl for a ride.

If you don't have a girl friend, a surfboard, or a belly-board, you might want to use a skim board. In an inch of water, a skim board will give you a good ride.

Is he going to shoot the pier? What style! What tempo! What trim!